Selected artworks, poems and short story entries from the

ENOUGH TO SEE
*but not enough to see by**

Competition 2023 curated by The Arts Society Worcester, Bevere Gallery, LitFest & Fringe and the Yew Trees Artists Studio and generously supported by Liberal Democrat Worcestershire County Councillor Mel Allcott.

In December 2022 the Yew Trees Artists, Bevere Gallery and Worcestershire LitFest & Fringe agreed to create a competition based on the theme **'Enough to See… *but not enough to see by'*.** Our aim was primarily to encourage creativity in the community but also to raise awareness of the work of our respective organisations. The Artwork strand was coordinated by Yew Trees Artists Jane Arthur, Susan Birth, Jennifer Ng and Bevere Gallery owner Kim Taylor. Martin Driscoll, a Worcestershire LitFest Director and published Flash Fiction author, coordinated the Writing strand.

In March 2023 we announced an Open Call to artists working in all media and poets and storytellers residing in Worcestershire to respond to the brief and the theme. We were delighted to receive so many amazing submissions and by the creativity of the artists and writers responding to our Open Call. Entries included paintings, drawings, multi-media pieces, textile art, photographs, poetry films, ceramics, poetry and music!

The final artworks for exhibition were selected by Yew Trees Artists Jane Arthur, Dan Holden, Jennifer Ng and Richard Nicholls together with Kim Taylor. Maggie Keeble, Chair of The Arts Society Worcester and two Arts Society members then chose the three prize-winning artworks. In addition, three 'highly commended' artworks were chosen by the Yew Trees Artists.

The written submissions were judged by Martin Driscoll and Emily Rose Galvin, the former Staffordshire Poet Laureate, who chose the three prize-winning poems and the 'highly commended' entries.

A number of the entries were inspired by the 'Enough to See' theme-based art of Susan, Dan, Jennifer, Jane and Richard and by the theme-based poems of five current or former Worcestershire Poets Laureate: Rhianna Levi, Leena Batchelor, Ade Couper, Nina Lewis and Suz Winspear.

In June 2023 we held a week-long Showcase Exhibition of the selected artworks and written pieces with the final Showcase Event on Saturday 17 June featuring live readings, prize-giving and music. The event was officially opened by Worcester's Deputy Mayor, Councillor Mel Allcott. The winners in the Art and Writing sections were presented with their prizes by Maggie Keeble, Chair of The Worcester Arts Society and Dr Mark Robbins, Chair of The Worcestershire LitFest & Fringe.

*'Enough to see but not enough to see by' is taken from the novel *House of Leaves* by Mark Danielewski.

The Yew Trees Studios artists' responses to the theme of Enough to See… but not enough to see by

Dystopian Undercurrent by Richard Nicholls
resident artist at Bevere
Original and manipulated Polaroid instant film

Elusive (2006) by Dan Holden
resident artist at Bevere
Two photographic images remembered and found again on discarded technology. Leading to thoughts on the transient nature of digital images

ENOUGH TO SEE **Page 1**

Ténèbres by Susan Birth
resident artist at Bevere
Mixed media on board

Secret Visibility: Walk by Jennifer Ng
resident artist at Bevere
Chinese ink and water-based medium

Avebury Imagined by Jane Arthur
resident artist at Bevere
Mixed media, textile and stitch

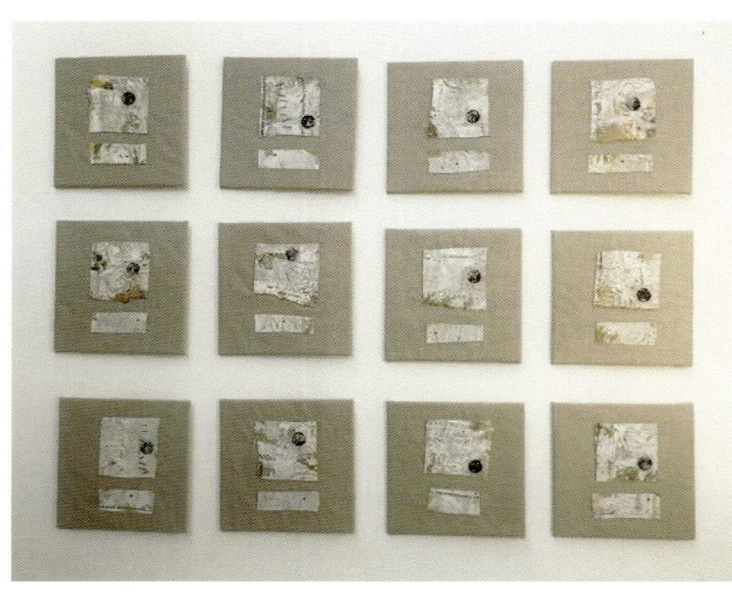

The Worcestershire Poets Laureate responses to the theme of *Enough to See... but not enough to see by*

Raindrop obscural

Sliding, dripping, melding with air raindrops gather incessantly upon the glass,
watched curiously, the lines they pulled through the clouds to find their rest
there drawn unseen from tremulous clouds,
hammered against fused silica and splintered wood, gravity-fuelled translucent lead
weights behind which I hide.

I missed your moments as they fell as tears upon your day.

I witnessed the sunrise, angry and bloodshot, resistant and hesitant against
my eyes, chased by the inevitability of a blazing sunset, and yet another,
and another,
endless cycles seen yet unnoticed in dreary repetition.

A single drop traces its wavering demise downwards,
subsumed by putty and wood as more and more pool
atop the ripple free lake of watery jewels.

I missed the moment to pause and see beneath the surface of your soul's lake.
Allowed the daylight to confuse senses and highlight the merest hint of you.

Trees now bend their branches to the coming storm, carrying your voice
in whispered breaths among the glistened leaves, brewing a broth
of fermenting realisation from the opaque greyness.

I feel each daylight beam, each moonrise droplet, upon my eyes,
and miss the shadow of what was there, now unseen among dancing dust motes
disturbed by fairy wings.

In the daylight, I look at sights but don't see patterns.
In the dark, with closed eyes, I see too much.

The windowpane, curtainless, gazes ahead at the stars, reflected
within sliding raindrops melting shadows,

hiding me from view,
hiding me from you

Leena Batchelor · Worcestershire Poet Laureate 2020-21

No stars

No stars.
There ought to be stars.

What little light there is—
enough to see,
not enough to see by—
comes from those far-away towns,
earth-made, not heavenly.

Still, I don't suppose it matters now.
Not now that you're gone.

No stars.

There ought to be stars...

Ade Couper · Worcestershire Poet Laureate 2021-22

Placemat Greed on Marbled Floor

Thoughts muddled across marble floor,
the breathing profile meanwhile
enraptured by gold specks
dropping in seeming blood bags full.
A result of absorbing golden coils that came
with life.

But that was not accordingly enough for
the presence at the door,
more adventures were wished to be
performed. And with that,
room to fusty room,
the effigy lust for oddities—amazements
not effortlessly clocked.
Not enough to have been seen by.

And as day met its end,
all that was left in a side room
with a vengeful chest,
were two glazed eyes of gold
that had met its wishful end.
Periodically, far too much has been seen.

Rhianna Levi
Worcestershire Poet Laureate 2022-23

Aperture

You lived through all the shadows,
a world at war and flowers cut
with new meaning.

You taught me how to write with light.
I run with it, like ribbons through the sky
I become child—kite,

whilst you close your eyes and trust darkness.
Breathe the luminosity
of stars. A single burn, brighter

than a galaxy of a billion.
We are only here for a small unit of time,
long enough to learn to see.

Nina Lewis
Worcestershire Poet Laureate 2017-18

Early Hours January

In the grudging crawl of a winter morning
time disconnects from clocks.
Dawn only comes reluctantly,
too late for the early riser
who stumbles through toe-stubbing gloom
between the bedroom and the shower.
Electric bulbs are not enough
to shift the sullen darkness
lingering to stain the day.
This dirty light allows for little clarity.
Outside, the garden blends its greys
with colours that can barely be distinguished,
merging into softness where the plants and trees
do not yet have the power
to differentiate themselves.
Beyond, the road is noisy
with the acting-out of morning,
of jobs to go to, business to attend,
while the real world keeps to shadows
and a careful fox slips
between the hedge and garden wall
to hurry home unseen.

Suz Winspear
Worcestershire Poet Laureate 2016-2017

The Word judges' responses to the theme of *Enough to See... but not enough to see by*

The Creeping Coastline
Martin Driscoll

As failing light gives up the ghost
and figures creep and loom
the spirit seeks its living host
it waits and haunts in gloom

It trawls along the promenade
and waves its empty cup
corrupted now, and crawling low
it longs to fill it up

The seas retreat
and leave that clinging shore,
sailors cannot see the lights
and sink for evermore

Once there was Enough to See,
and seas enough to steer…
But soon no dock is safe to berth
that ailing, wounded ship
and something wrong is near

And now the coast's not clear
as monsters come at last
we turn to face our darkest fear

The die has now been cast

This poem is inspired by 'Creeping Coastline of Light' by Mark Lanegan and by Susan Birth's artwork 'Ténèbres'

Viola
Emily Rose Galvin

And now the day
begins to crack,
spills its evening yolk
across the creases in the sky,
and still

    those little faces stand attentive

and earnest.
A tiny, white chorus
spreading up against the green.

I am not bright enough
to be your sun
I say,
fold in
and save your
pretty little faces
from the dark.

Our solar brushed bodies
flame against the cooling,
but still
those pretty little faces
remain unyielding
and bright
as we glow unknowing
into the dusk.

But there is light
they say
Don't you see?
There is still so much light.

Emily Rose Galvin is a former Staffordshire Poet Laureate (2017-2019), former Poet in Residence at Lichfield Library and co-founder of Stoke-on-Trent spoken word organisation WordCraft.

"Viola' takes its inspiration from both the natural world and human nature, and the ways in which we can become blind to our own virtues and positivity, though these attributes may be clear for others to see. The theme of 'light' was prevalent throughout the written entries for the Enough to See project, and this piece draws focus in to our own internal light and energy, through the perspective of an audience of flowers.

FIRST PRIZE WINNERS
ART AND WORDS

'Woven Apertures'
by Sally Cartwright
First prize
Scrap yarns, recycled plastic pot lid looms

These 20 mini weaves are each 'apertures' created by recreating a section of a cut up photograph taken on one of my favourite walks in the Worcestershire countryside. The apertures represent a portal from my everyday life, as are the walks, transporting me to the textures of the countryside.

'Reflect'
by Rachel Porter
First prize

Reflect

Each night I find him
wrapped tightly in soft cotton sheeting,
softly bleating
in the corner of the room.

In these small hours,
in the alien glow of a digital clock,
I have sat in a chair I could not swear was there in daylight.

I have held him gently in my creaking hands
and seen myself as a weathered monument to my own strength,
as a cracked cliff face to which tender plants cling,
a leaking vessel of rusted metal.

Then, in the pitch lack of his bright unseeing eyes
I have seen a brutalist sculpture
Woman in a New Light.
Lumpen, unfamiliar, pale as concrete,
yet human in form.

SECOND PRIZE WINNERS
ART AND WORDS

'Transpired'
by Charli Farquharson
Second prize
Acrylic on canvas

With no singular meaning, my artwork echoes that of the book from which the quotation was taken. A labyrinth of implications are drawn from the canvas, from the darkness, the shadows, the brilliance and the understanding. Atmospheric-loss, half-remembered ideas glimpsed, horror, love, loss; the choice is with the beholder.

'Age related Macular Degeneration'
by Angela Lanyon
Second prize

Age related Macular Degeneration

Now, although I cannot see the stars
I know they're there.
The stars remain beyond the canopy of cloud,
visible by day to those who've trained
and know the place to look.
The crescent moon was once a sliver scythe
to reap the sky—
a crooked notice hanging on a star.

CLOSED.

I still see things.
Honeycombs, magenta, pink and green
with cream surround (but rarely red or blue)
tumbleweed twinkling spheres
that whizz off into space like Catherine wheels.
I see dead bodies on the TV screen,
rubble from earthquakes, damage in Ukraine,
tear-rivered faces rubbed with grubby hands.
'Tell me your name?' I ask the friends I meet.

I see enough—enough to know
that through the smoke and mirrors of my life
the stars remain.

THIRD PRIZE WINNERS ART AND WORDS

Light as a Dragonfly' by Sylvie Millen

Third prize

Free-motion machine stitched art/mixed media

The dragonfly, a spiritual symbol of transformation and lightness, it's quickness of flight and translucent wings, a reminder of the wonders of nature, spirituality and the meaning of life. My lightly stitched free-motion embroidery work tries to capture a vision of a dream-like world, a monochromatic impression of the moment, where my imagination and reality blur into one.

'Observations Following His Confinement'
by Brian Comber
Third prize

Observations Following His Confinement

Then ten years in the attic,
Van Hoeken felt the earth's daily tilt, sleep rise and fall
upon his chest, the hollow in his pillow, the scurf on his counterpane,
the systole and diastole of his house of decline.

He knew when snow settled without opening his eyes,
the factory klaxon marked the seasons, the thin slant
from the louvres varied as winter approached; he laid down fat
for the lean months, he wanted spectacles but no one came.

Mosquitos swam from the vast Brownian exosphere
of perfumed sweat, his slab of heat a beacon, more blood than flesh;
he called for drape nets, insecticides to purge the gloom
peered then waited, with not enough light to see.

Curled in his feverish dreams, neutrinos perforated the earth,
trillions of luminescent bursts lit his riddled body,
as the cosmos patiently ran
cells bloomed in his macula, scarred his cornea like sandpaper;

his eyesight crazed as the world of light dimmed,
insufficient to see his books, his pail, his unopened mail,
the diminishing spectrum faded to infra-red.
He called and indistinct figures gathered about his bed.

HIGHLY COMMENDED ART AND WORDS

'Awaiting'
by Nashmin Riazi

Highly commended
Mixed media abstract

Waiting for anyone or anything, to bring passion. I am always inspired by shapes and movements that are naturally created in my abstract work.

The texture of this painting is made with different materials such as crack paste and acrylic paste. I have used acrylic paint on a hand-stretched canvas before varnishing.

Moonpaths

Rain clouds clear from the night sky,
moonlight glistens on the wet tarmac.
I walk on, drinking in the unexpected beauty…

As I walk, my footsteps slow once more,
stop and listen—
the night is full of magical moonpaths.

Background to the music:

This piece has been written for a pedal harp, an instrument which is the only one in Western Classical tradition which allows the player to set two strings to the same note and change the tuning during performance; this is known as enharmonic pedalling.

Extreme keys and tuning tricks are used to create a moonlit landscape in sound.

ENOUGH TO SEE Page 12

'Moonpaths'
by Jan Scarrot
Highly commended

Moonpaths
Enough to See... But Not Enough to See By
For Solo Harp

Jan Scarrott

Fix G Sharp
E Natural

HIGHLY COMMENDED ART AND WORDS

'It's Just a Mouse' by Gary Williams

Highly commended

Lino print

Occasionally we fished with Dad through the night. He was brave, but he didn't like the rustles and crashes in the undergrowth. If we asked *what was that?* he would say *'It's just a mouse'*. But he would never turn around to look. But what if it wasn't a mouse?

'When I Remember'
by Charli Farquharson
Highly commended

When I Remember

I am here
aren't you? My sweet?

I can hear you touch me
I can smell the taste of your sweat
tonguing down my neck
I know you are here, glistening in the moonlight.

Your footsteps lay flattened
the carpet you tread
back and forth, back and forth, aye,
and I know you are here
your smile fast upon your face
and laughing

every

single

time

I close my eyes to go to sleep
you are laughing silently for me
my arms crying out in strangled mourning.

Is that you breathing through the rain?
Can I hear your breath?
Just
listening, I can feel the heat touching my neck
hot and close and so very, very far…
still
I know I can hear you through the rain that falls on your face.
Pitter patters, pitters pats.

Is that your hand I can see?
Tired without holding onto mine,
weary and watching
looking in the place we once were
but no longer gather,
finding and finishing,

I know you.

HIGHLY COMMENDED ART AND WORDS

'Looking Enough to See' by Juliet May

Highly commended

Digital drawing

The figures are young and trying to see and make sense of something, perhaps searching for meaning. The challenge of making sense of life is a universal experience but often our vision is obstructed by unnecessary clutter.

'Enough to See...
but not enough to see by'
by Matt Trobe
Highly commended

Enough to See...but not enough to see by

I was putting my 10-year-old daughter to bed. There was a small nightlight in the room,
Enough to See...but not enough to see by.
'Dad, I'm frightened.' She whispered as I stroked her head. 'What if I come last in the sports day tomorrow?'
'What if you come first?' was my reply.

'To be successful you have to lean in' Sheryl Sandberg said.
Over dinner that night I leant in to show I was listening
and got tomato ketchup on my shirt.
I leant back out again and made a mental note.
To listen from a distance. To listen enough to hear
but not enough to get hurt.

The next day we headed off to school.
My daughter was in running, jumping and the egg and spoon.
I found a spot where I could see
and prayed she would at least be in the middle.
Each time, the gun fired and off they went.
To my relief and shock, she won. All three.

Our futures are all made up stories,
our past, at best, a personal view.
So what's the soundtrack as we live our life?
Are we guided by the shadows or reflections
of Macbeth's brief candle or Shaw's flaming torch?
Well, it's enough to see but not enough to see by.

My wife and I had a disagreement last night.
'Just because I'm shouting and you are all calm,
doesn't mean you are right' she said.
At work they told us there are five levels of listening.
I can't remember the last two. My mind was wandering.
But I conceded she had a fair point as we lay in bed.

It was night-time and silent in the Donetsk Orphanage
when the siren started. Then came the bombs.
'Everybody up. To the cellar now. Walk quickly. Don't fly.'
In the gloom, Mary touched the head of each child.
As she counted them safe, the candlelight was enough to see,
and was enough to see by.

HIGHLY COMMENDED ART AND WORDS

'Waiting'
by Gillian Swan
Highly commended
Mixed media

A train platform on a late summer evening after a day of exploring. The smell of the metal bench after being heated by the sun. The fading light washing colour away.

'I Cast Two Shadows'
by Jay Rose Ana
Highly commended

I Cast Two Shadows

I cast two shadows, one of you and one of me,
both filled with horrors and harrows, too much to see.
A rabbit hole, a labyrinth, a chamber of secrets,
lost in darkness, with only love to guide me
 and you to me.

As I follow distant light, two shadows walk with me
flickering in the candlelight
never pulling away, never needing to stray,
they are where I have always
 needed them to be.

I cast two shadows, one of you and one of me,
both filled with hope and humility, not enough to see.
Through life and love and endless why's,
lost in darkness, with only love to guide me
 and you to me.

HIGHLY COMMENDED ART AND WORDS

'Fathomage'
by Heather Mason

Highly commended

This piece is a response to the artwork 'Secret Visibility: Walk' by Jennifer Ng.

Mixed media on cotton rag paper

It also addresses the theme of subjective perspectives. My subject is an interpretation of the distortions induced by the dynamic, ever-changing fluidity of water in a stream, where one's view of the stream bed remains singular, elusive and ultimately indeterminate.

'Multiverse'
by Lauren Pizzicaroli
Highly commended

Multiverse

Somewhere out there is another version of me
climbing to the peak of a mountain in February.
And somewhere out there is another version of me

where I'm the lead singer in a world-famous boy band,
another version where I'm thin and walk the runway,
and another where I'm a hot dog eating champion.

Another where I dodge bullets in kung-fu slow motion,
and another where I've won a Nobel Prize for keeping peace.
Somewhere out there is another version of me

that's more successful, smarter, skilled,
living their life to their full potential.
But for now, they are invisible

and all that exists here is me
wondering if I am enough, wondering
if I am enough for you to see.

OTHER SELECTED WORKS

'Like Ribbons through the Sky'
by Cherrie Mansfield

Acrylic on canvas

Look closely and you catch a glimpse of the inspiration behind this work peeping through the dynamic multi-layers of paint. The piece explores themes and rhythms from the second and third verses of 'Woven Aperture': writing with light, becoming child, trusting darkness and breathing the luminosity of stars.

The Hiding Corner

Beyond the bend is where I can no longer make amends.
I am forgetting why I am here...Is it out of fear?
The gravel cries out as I crunch each step.
Leaves taunt me, the wind knocks me down.
I'd like to believe there is something beyond, glistening, shining.
Something that transcends me out...out from...out...
I am living one step behind, moving yet never going forward.
Listening to the birds singing, yet just hearing white noise.
Hoping for more behind the hidden corner, yet simply turning back.
Wanting to be there for them, yet I'm choosing to walk the path alone

One foot is off the ground ready to shift, where do I place it?

'The Hiding Corner'
by Wesley Rolston

'Amber Revelation'
by Jan Husband

Oil paint blended with cold wax

The artwork depicts the descriptive light of sunset; in which some colours are enhanced and others diminished to dark shapes. The image is in homage to the poem by Emily Dickenson: 'An Ignorance - a Sunset' in which she coins the term 'an amber revelation.'

'Who has Never Killed an Hour?'
by Clare Knighton

Who has Never Killed an Hour?

Where do the sparrows go at night?
Silent wing and absent flight.
Pigeons who in day annoy and coo,
can't be seen in darkness new.
The setting sun, a light so dim
hides the wildlife held within.
Pause, stop, look and sigh,
spend an hour, let time pass by
for who has never killed an hour
watching wildlife, nature's power?

'Dawn Robin'
by Jessica Pahl
Oil on canvas

Dawn

I sit outside.
A robin catches my eye.
I look at it,
it looks at me.
A mythical creature bringing a message
from a spirit recently departed?
Or just a dawn robin?
It gives me enough time to wonder,
but not enough to decide, before flitting away
into the night.

'Enough to See...
but not enough to see by'
by Paula Pearson

Enough to See...but not enough to see by

What do you see when you look at me?
Do you SEE me, or the person I strive to be?
Do you see a curvy woman, who waddles when she walks,
notice my accent when my mouth opens and talks?
Know where I come from and what I do?
Does it even matter to you?
I come across happy, confident and social,
but in truth, in my life, I've been very emotional.
I've seen things I wish I hadn't have seen,
been around people I shouldn't have been.
I feel like I've been through hell and back too,
there is an awful lot that I have been through;
looked after my mum when I was just nine
who suffers with MS, but was once fine.
My parents divorced, I left home at 16,
split from my partner, who was really mean.
Nearly was homeless, but luckily got by,
many times in my life where I'd just sit and cry.
Fibromyalgia and other aches and pains,
all contribute to my daily strains.
Things are not all doom and gloom,
I found my soulmate, who became my groom.
13 years on we are stronger than ever;
with a son and two daughters, who we truly treasure.
So, don't prejudge someone by just using sight,
get to know them—then SEE them properly, you might...

'Face'
by Lucy Turner

Graphite and charcoal

This artwork is a response to the poem Raindrop Obscural by Leena Batchelor

In my drawing I have tried to capture feelings of loss and sorrow and give the impression of a detached observer watching life pass by behind a veil of regret.

'Quest for Clarity'
by David Oliver

Quest for Clarity

We seek direction, to reach a place where we feel that we belong,
to live a life in a flow that runs smoothly, be at ease with the world and spend our energy on that which we choose to rather than have to.
It is not always so simple, sometimes it seems so difficult that we know not which way to turn, leaving us feeling that nothing will change
and questioning our motivation to discover a path to follow.
The mists of time hinder the clarity desired to be certain of what is yet to come,
so that we may be prepared to take on and overcome whatever challenges should arise to be conquered.
It is not what we are looking at, but the way in which we perceive the view and if we move our perspective to a higher plane and ascend
to clear skies, we shall become aligned with a clear vision.

'Placemat Greed on Marbled Floor' by Caroline Hall

Etching and acrylics

This artwork is a response to the poem of the same title by Rhianna Levi

I was inspired by Rhianna's poem and decided to use an etching as I felt the black and white imagery was perfect for the poem's morbid tone. Acrylics were applied to the print to highlight those elements of the poem which I understood to be important.

'Under a Rainbow'
by Paul Smith

Under a Rainbow

While standing under this colourful rainbow, I long for your embrace.
At this unforeseen moment, I grow not strong in faith.
We should embrace our love together and flourish entwined,
we'd be among spring's bright, colourful surroundings,
get to know each other well.
For all time, we two could celebrate the talents and gifts of heaven
that lie within our wake.
Throughout life's long and short journeys we may well stumble upon
its deep and hidden secrets that lie in wait for us to come upon;
both caring for one another in sickness and health.
We can live together and amuse ourselves with song,
look forward to the future and many happy years to come,
brighten one another's lives with inspiration and insight,
support each other's ventures and encounters and look back
at what we've done.
Like the deep and wondrous oceans we get to know each other
without shame,
seek for peace within the country to be independent and so strong,
forever in the sight of the holy father and blessed by his mighty hand.
Entwined within our wedlock too, wholeheartedly combined.

Nothing Left to See - a poetry film by Kathy Gee
https://vimeo.com/838224651

'Nothing Left to See'
by Kathy Gee

Stills from a poetry film

In poetry film, images work best as metaphors for what the words are saying. This creates a fluid dialogue between the two which enriches the meaning. In real life, 'experience' is a combination of all the senses, but when we tell someone else, we inevitably experience it in words.

'Nothing Left to See'
by Kathy Gee

Nothing Left to See

Doorways are a promise, framing time
where outdoors leads to indoors, where the daylight
of today explores the dark of then.

Along my road, I've stumbled on the threshold
of your story, tumbled relics of long years in ruins.
Somehow, weathered stones are not enough
to tell me how the past was lived when you
were young. You're gone. There's nothing left to see.

No doors remain to keep this stranger out;
protective walls of plastered comfort have been
stripped away by years of rain. Your life
once blazed across these floors, but who you were
back then is dark and dead. A room is not
a home when every scrap of light has gone.

'Crepuscular'
by Jim Hanlon
Acrylic on canvas

My painting Crepuscular is my visual response to the project theme. It's composed with a monochromatic and low level of colour and light similar to nautical twilight. The word-based theme led me to include elements of implied narrative, a moment in time which hints at an unresolved story.

'Web Prints of Worcester's Past' by Paul Grime

Web Prints of Worcester's Past

The Butts, The Butts
just outside the ancient city walls
where archers arrowed
and now the railway arches across the Severn
and one-way arrows shoot buses up The Butts
towards their target (CrownGate Bus Station)
approaching Sansome Street (formerly Town Ditch)
stopping short of Lansdowne Road (formerly Cut Throat Lane)
and when the Severn bursts her banks and becomes a lake again
Sabrina, goddess from an age of iron and ironing
spills and spirits herself around the Pitchcroft and up the High Street
and without sound or song
monastic swans snub sanctuary
ignore the one-way system
disrespect the public library
and the shiny university buildings
the blue plaques where Elgar
went to school/took violin lessons/ate breakfast/died
pass by the Asda trolley beak down in the canal
and saunter into the Cathedral
where Oswald and Wulfstan
bishoped around
like they knew
what swans know

To See Beyond

Does not see it, so does not say it

To think it, but unable to say it

Does not think it, so cannot say it

To say it and not mean it

Does see it, but refuses to say it

To say it and mean every word of it

About my work and how it links to the theme

We take a risk when expressing our feelings. At what point have we seen enough for us to comment? What does this look like? How do we measure 'enough'?

This poem recognises the complexities associated with communicating how we feel in response to what we see before us.

'To See Beyond'
by Katie Joyce